Positive Recruitment and Retention

OTHER BOOKS WITHIN THIS SERIES

Using Information for Decision-Making	0750664274
Developing Personal Potential	0750664231
Creating a Customer Focus	0750664266
Maximizing Resources	075066424X
Improving Competitive Advantage	0750664258
Successful Project Management	0750664193
Developing High Performance Teams	0750664207
Successful Project Management	0750664193
Communication in Organizations	0750664282

POSITIVE RECRUITMENT AND RETENTION

Author: Corinne Leech

Series Editor: Kate Williams

AMSTERDAM • BOSTON • HEIDELBERG • LONDON • OXFORD • NEW YORK • PARIS • SAN DIEGO • SAN FRANCISCO • SINGAPORE • SYDNEY • TOKYO

Elsevier Butterworth-Heinemann
Linacre House, Jordan Hill, Oxford OX2 8DP
30 Corporate Drive, Burlington, MA 01803

First published 2005

British Library Cataloguing in Publication Data
A catalogue record for this book is available from the British Library

ISBN 0 7506 6422 3

For information on all Elsevier Butterworth-Heinemann publications visit our website at http://books.elsevier.com

Typeset by Charon Tec Pvt. Ltd, Chennai, India
Printed and bound in Italy

Contents

Series overview

The Chartered Management Institute Flexible Learning programme is a series of workbooks prepared by the Chartered Management Institute and Elsevier for managers seeking to develop themselves.

Comprising ten open learning workbooks, the programme covers the best of modern management theory and practice. Each workbook provides a range of frameworks and techniques to improve your effectiveness as a manager, thus helping you acquire the knowledge and skill to make you fully competent in your role.

Each workbook is written by an experienced management writer and covers an important management topic or theme. The activities both reinforce learning and help to relate the generic ideas to your individual work context. While coverage of each topic is fully comprehensive, additional reading suggestions and reference sources are given for those who wish to study in greater depth.

Designed to be practical, stimulating and challenging, the aim of the workbooks is to improve performance at work by benefiting you and your organization. This practical focus is at the heart of the competence-based approach that has been adopted by the programme.

Introduction

Most organizations recognize that their staff provide the bedrock on which success is built.

> Effective, efficient, well-motivated staff = Success for any organization

The equation has to include the staff at all levels of the organization and depends on the quality of staff appointed to the organization.

The recruitment and selection process is made up of two main stages:

- **Recruitment** – this involves all the steps which result in applications being received
- **Selection** – this is about identifying a person for the job from the applicants.

Labour turnover is a costly process.

Cost of labour turnover

The overall average cost of turnover per employee in 2001 was £3462. (Managers have the highest costs per leaver at £5699.)

It is difficult to calculate the average cost of labour turnover, as organizations use different methods and measures. However, the costs will primarily cover:

- **Leaving** – payroll and personnel administration for the leaver
- **Replacement** – recruitment, interview time and placement fees
- **Transition** – training costs, reduced performance while learning and during induction
- **Indirect** – loss in customer service/satisfaction.

(Source: *Labour Turnover 2002*, Survey Report, Chartered Institute of Personnel and Development, www.cipd.org.uk)

Recruiting the wrong person brings additional costs and problems. For example:

- You will need to spend your time sorting things out
- They will be an increased burden on the rest of your team
- Loss in customer service/satisfaction will be prolonged
- The recruitment and selection process may have to be repeated.

Therefore, getting it right the first time, and not incurring any costly mistakes, is essential.

The way you handle recruitment and selection has to:

- be set within the framework of your organization's policies and procedures
- meet legal requirements.

It should also reflect recognition of the business benefits of diversity within your team and the wider organization. Therefore, this workbook begins by exploring the wider concept of diversity and equal opportunities before looking in detail at the stages within the recruitment and selection process.

Objectives

By the end of this workbook you should be better able to:

- recognize the degree of commitment to diversity in your organization
- check your attitudes towards valuing diversity
- consider the advantages of a diverse workforce to your team and your organization
- understand the main purpose of equal opportunities legislation in the recruitment and selection process
- identify the selection methods which are most appropriate to the appointment of members of your team
- update job descriptions and person specification for your team
- manage the recruitment process
- make selection decisions based on an objective assessment of evidence
- provide a good induction to new members of your team
- recognize the importance of managing your team's performance on retention.

Section 1 Diversity, equality and the law

Introduction

Understanding diversity is an essential prerequisite for managing the recruitment and selection process. A mindset which actively values diversity will shape all aspects of the process and bring benefits to your team and organization.

In this section we look at what is meant by diversity, its benefits and its relationship to the concept of equality of opportunity and the 'equal opportunity legislation'. We also begin to explore the barriers some people may have towards creating diverse teams as it's commonly recognized that people feel more comfortable selecting people in their own image.

What does diversity in the workplace mean?

Few people would dispute that every single person is unique; different in some ways to everyone else. Therefore, it could be argued that any group of people is diverse.

However, diversity in the workplace is about selecting people who bring in a *wide* variety of backgrounds and experiences due to differences in their:

- inherited characteristics (i.e. age, ethnicity, gender, sexual orientation)
- culture (the way of doing things we feel comfortable with).

Our culture results from the way we were brought up and live. It's a result of our life experiences – something we acquire, develop and can modify throughout our lives. It includes our personal values and beliefs, routines and preferences.

ACTIVITY 1

List four factors which can affect a person's culture.

FEEDBACK

You may have included:

- family beliefs and values
- educational background
- religious beliefs
- geographic location
- friends and colleagues
- work experience.

Inherited characteristics (nature) and our culture (nurture) combine to form the uniqueness of individuals.

Nature + Nurture = Behaviour/personality, i.e. what you are like

The debate around how much we're affected by 'nature' and 'nurture' rages on amongst scientists.

'The finding that we have far fewer genes than expected suggests that environmental influences play a greater role in our development than was previously thought'

(Source: *Nature or nurture?* Science/Nature, Sunday 11 February 2004, http://news.bbc.co.uk)

What's important to understand is that diversity at work isn't just about race or gender. It's about recognizing and valuing that people are different from each other and adapting workplace practices accordingly.

DIVERSITY AT WORK

'A strategy to promote values, behaviour and working practices which recognize the difference between people and thereby enhance staff motivation and performance and release potential, delivering improved service to customers'[1]

The starting point for any organization must be to make sure that the result of the recruitment and selection process is to appoint employees from diverse backgrounds into the organization.

ACTIVITY 2

Consider the senior management within your organization. How diverse are the people related to the factors listed below? Mark where you think they fall on a continuum between being very similar at one end and diverse at the other.

	Very similar	**Diverse**
Age		
Gender		
Ethnicity		
Educational background		
Religious beliefs		
Physical ability/disabilities		
Previous work experiences		

Now consider your team. How diverse is it in relation to the same factors?

	Very similar	Diverse
Age		
Gender		
Ethnicity		
Educational background		
Religious beliefs		
Physical ability/disabilities		
Previous work experiences		

FEEDBACK

There has been a considerable shift in attitudes and practice in recent years from compliance with equal opportunity legislation to embracing diversity at work. However, that diversity has yet to percolate into many boardrooms and levels of senior management. For example:

> *'The global business community has taken too long to realise the power of releasing the intellectual capital of women in leadership'*
>
> Jack Smith, Chairman of General Motors

The business case for diversity

The move towards valuing diversity involves more than the drive towards social justice. A diverse workforce makes good business sense for organizations. Many organizations are recognizing the dangers of having a workforce who come from similar backgrounds.

The disastrous launch of the Space Shuttle *Challenger* on 28 January 1986 is attributed, in part, to the homogeneous company culture of the decision makers – male engineers with identical engineering backgrounds and similar personality profiles. The NASA managers were so hell-bent on reaching their objectives that they ignored safety warnings from outside contractors. Because NASA managers were so similar in background they developed a 'group mentality' which overrode good judgment. Only bringing in a significant number of managers who are not in the 'NASA mould' would the much needed diversity to the team be added.[2]

Adapted from *Management Focus Issue 12, Summer 1999*, Cranfield School of Management.

They are also recognizing the benefits that a diverse workforce brings. In a survey[3] of more than a hundred of the UK's leading organizations:

- Eighty per cent of all respondents said they saw a direct link between diversity and business performance. Of the responses from private sector companies, 71 per cent saw the link between diversity and performance compared with 87 per cent of public sector respondents
- Successful equality and diversity policies deliver significant business benefits including: better recruitment, increased retention, improved understanding of markets and communities, an enhanced reputation and cost savings.

AstraZeneca – global pharmaceutical company:

We employ over 60,000 people worldwide with a wide variety of backgrounds, experience and skills – our diversity is one of our core values and a natural source of energy and creativity.

Our definition of diversity includes all our different personal skills and qualities as well as race and gender, where advancement depends solely on ability, performance and good teamwork. Across the business, diversity is high on the agenda and continuous improvement is at the heart of our approach. And we have a clear focus on the future – an aspiration to become a true culture of diversity.

(Source: www.astrazeneca.com, July 2004)

'Achieving excellence in diversity is one of the marks of a truly world-class company, and is one of Barclay's core values. My time as Chief Executive has proved to me that diversity is not a 'nice to have' but a significant part of the answer to our business challenges. Attracting the brightest and best people from all backgrounds, bringing a richness of experience and knowledge to the workplace, and improving our understanding of our increasingly diverse customer-base simply makes good business sense'

Matt Barrett, Barclays Group Chief Executive

For construction company Durkan Ltd., employing women has resulted in several benefits for the company, including: positive publicity that has boosted the company's brand image by meeting the cultural ethos of organizations that give the organization work, as well as appealing to a growing number of female managers who are in a position to offer building contracts. The company insists that the bottom line for employing women is that they can do the job. 'We have employed many women on-site over the years. The reason we choose to do so is because they have proven that they can do the work and do it well. We are a commercial company not a charity. If women were not up to the job then we would not hire them.'[4]

(Source: *Equal Opportunities Review*, 129, 1/5/2004)

Emphasis on the importance of reflecting a diverse customer base is particularly important for businesses in the service sector.

Fiona Cannon, Head of Equality and Diversity at Lloyds TSB, when asked about the costs of ensuring a more diverse workforce, stated that:

'There are costs, of course there are costs, but you know a lot of it is around just doing things differently. So, for example, if you're recruiting and you've traditionally advertised in a certain number of publications, you know you might want to change some of those publications to reach a broader market of people. Similarly, if you're looking at graduate recruitment, if you've always gone to the same universities – for example where you know that there's largely a white population of graduates – then you might want to look at going to some other universities that have a broader range of candidates there. So that doesn't necessarily mean there's a cost; it's just about a different way of allocating resources. If we're losing people because they don't believe the organization is serious about diversity, then that's a much bigger worry to us and completely offsets the cost of any work that we might do on women's development or ethnic minority development, for example. When we looked at our customer side of it, again there are very few

(*Continued*)

direct costs around that. For example, one of our North London areas looked at changing the composition of its workforce so it reflected more closely the community, and in one year it had a huge growth in sales as a result of that work and went from being one of the lowest performing parts of the business to one of the top performing parts of the business'

(Source: Extract from *Analysis*, BBC Radio 4, 2/9/04 BBC copyright (Tel 020 8752 6252))

Therefore, valuing diversity makes good business sense as well as being based on moral considerations for a fairer society.

ACTIVITY 3

Research by the Society for Human Resource Management (www.shrm.org) identifies the following thirteen advantages of committing to a diverse workforce. Consider each one and decide if you see it as a competitive advantage which is:

- relevant to your organization
- directly relevant to your team

		Your organization	Your team
1	Improves corporate culture	❏	❏
2	Improves employee morale	❏	❏
3	Enables higher retention of employees	❏	❏
4	Facilitates easier recruitment of employees	❏	❏
5	Decreases complaints and litigation	❏	❏
6	Increases creativity	❏	❏
7	Decreases interpersonal conflict between employees	❏	❏
8	Enables the organization to move into emerging markets	❏	❏
9	Improves client relations	❏	❏
10	Increases productivity	❏	❏
11	Improves the bottom line	❏	❏
12	Maximizes brand identity	❏	❏
13	Reduces training costs	❏	❏

FEEDBACK

The relevance to your organization or team of each of the factors will depend on your specific situation. In the research undertaken by the Society for Human Resource Management, over 60 per cent of the top Fortune companies identified the top five factors listed above as benefits resulting from diversity in their workforce.

Achieving a diverse workforce

The business case for diversity is well-established. However, putting it into practice requires:

- an organizational strategy
- individual managers to have a mindset which actively values diversity.

ORGANIZATIONAL STRATEGY

Any recruitment and selection process has to be integrated within a wider organizational strategy. Research[3] has highlighted that organizations which are serious about diversity adopt a four stage process:

1. Explicitly considering diversity in overall objective setting and business planning
2. Using existing business process for integration (e.g. integration within recruitment and selection process; work-life balance initiatives)
3. Measurement (e.g. diversity scorecards, specifying targets and goals)
4. Accountability (68 per cent of organizations reported that they had processes to hold managers accountable; only 27 per cent linked this to pay).

ACTIVITY 4

You may need to talk to the Human Resources department to answer this activity.

Has your organization got a diversity policy? Yes ❑ No ❑

If yes:

1 Can you identify examples of how the policy has been translated into processes? Yes ❑ No ❑

2 How is the diversity of the workforce measured?

3 Are managers held accountable? Yes ❑ No ❑

If yes, how?

FEEDBACK

You will be able to draw your conclusions as to how seriously your organization embraces diversity in its workforce. Research has shown that two years of a comprehensive approach to integration which leaves no area of the business untouched, is likely to have more of an affect than twenty years of piecemeal change.

Checking your mindset

Everyone has their own 'comfort zone'; we tend to feel comfortable with what we're used to. Change is seen as a threat and anything different can seem 'odd' or irrelevant. Therefore, people's resistance to change can pose a major barrier to valuing diversity at work.

If you don't change your beliefs, your life will be like this forever. Is that good news?

Douglas Adams, *Hitchhikers Guide to the Galaxy*

Attitudes towards people we perceive as being 'different' can also cause barriers. An attitude is the way we think or feel about a person. Our attitudes are influenced by our needs, feelings and beliefs. They help us to make sense of the world and tend to affect the way we behave.

People's attitudes are a result of a variety of factors which include:

- the way they live and were brought up (i.e. a person's culture)
- the messages they receive from the media (e.g. television, newspapers)
- knowledge, or lack of, about a particular topic.

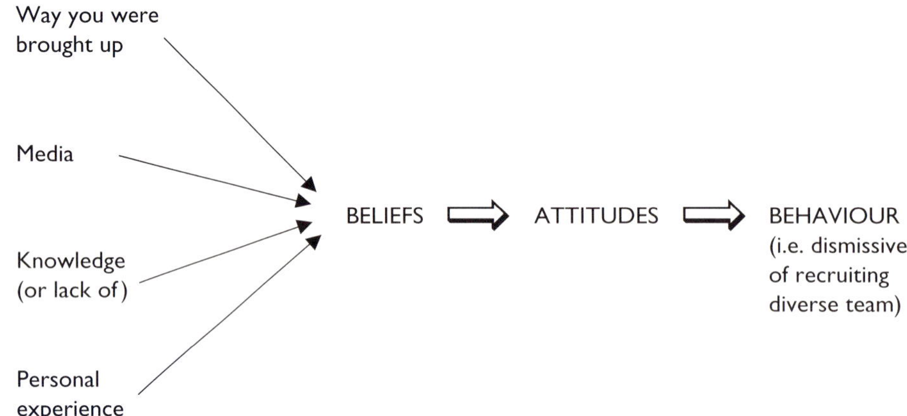

Figure 1.1 Influences which drive our attitudes

ACTIVITY 5

Typical attitudes of non-disabled people towards people with disabilities include pity, embarrassment, fear of not behaving appropriately and curiosity.

Identify two factors in society which have contributed towards people developing these attitudes.

FEEDBACK

You may have thought of:

- lack of personal experience or knowledge
- messages in the news media that reinforce images of disabled people as needy, grateful, deserving, plucky or brave. These images underline ideas that disabled people are separate from non-disabled people
- charities – in raising money they give prominence to differences and show that people with disabilities need help
- the way children with disabilities used to be segregated from mainstream schools.

Attitudes based on these beliefs are likely to result in a manager being dismissive of the capabilities of an applicant with a disability. In other words, prejudice, based on unfounded beliefs, leads to discriminatory behaviour.

Unlearning attitudes which lead to discrimination involves challenging the beliefs. This is not easy. The very nature of a belief is that it is right – that it is a fact of life.

The only way that you check your assumptions about what is normal or acceptable is to ask yourself the questions:

- *Why do I think that?*
- *What makes my way better?*
- *Could I explain to someone else why my way is better?*

A narrow view of what is normal or acceptable does not stand up to close scrutiny. Being able to value diversity means being able to widen your view of what is normal to include the rich diversity of human life.

ACTIVITY 6

In Activity 2 you were asked to consider the extent of diversity within your team. To what extent do you feel that your attitudes towards the following factors have either helped or hinder the diversity in your team?

- Your attitude towards change

- Your attitude towards valuing and accepting difference in other people

FEEDBACK

Attitudes are extremely personal. However, as a manager, it's important to be able to manage the change to increased diversity in the workplace. This may demand a rigorous reassessment of your own beliefs and attitudes.

Diversity and equality

Valuing diversity in the workplace is a relatively recent concept. Equality has been around a lot longer.

FROM DISCRIMINATION TO EQUALITY OF OPPORTUNITY

In the second half of the twentieth century, society's attitudes towards groups of people who were discriminated against (i.e. treated less favourably than others) began to change. For example:

From	→	**Towards**
Social isolation and segregation of people with disabilities	→	Greater integration/independent living
Blatant discrimination against people from black and minority ethnic groups	→	Less discrimination, e.g. in terms of employment
Expectation that a woman's place was 'in the home'	→	Women recognized as having equal potential to men in the job market
Non-existence of rights for couples in same sex relationships	→	Less discrimination, e.g. some organizations giving the same pension rights to same sex couples

These momentous social changes were driven mainly by demands for social justice, and the changes increased expectations across society until gradually there was recognition that:

1. there is discrimination in society
2. it is unacceptable.

This led to legislation being passed to outlaw some types of discrimination. For example, in the UK:

- Equal Pay Act, 1970. This law prevents unjustifiable differences between the pay of men and women
- Sex Discrimination Act, 1975. Outlaws discrimination on the grounds of gender
- The Race Relations Act, 1976 (Amended 2000). Outlaws discrimination on grounds of racial background in areas such as employment, education and the provision of goods and services
- Disability Discrimination Act, 1995. Outlaws discrimination against disabled people in employment and the provision of services
- Human Rights Act, 1998. States that 'the enjoyment of rights and freedoms shall be secured without discrimination on any ground such as sex, race, colour, language, religion, political or other opinion, national or social origin, association with a national minority, property, birth or other status'
- European Directive, 2000. Covers employment and training. It prohibits discrimination on grounds of sexual orientation, religion, disability and age.

WHAT DOES OUTLAWING DISCRIMINATION IN RECRUITMENT AND SELECTION MEAN IN PRACTICE?

Outlawing discrimination involves giving everyone equal access to services and opportunities. In practice, this can mean giving people the *same treatment*. For example:

Discrimination	→	**Outlawing discrimination means that**
A black applicant applies for a job. The application is rejected because the applicant is black and therefore wouldn't 'fit in'	→	The ethnicity of a person is not a factor at any stage of the selection process
A woman applies for a job and is rejected because it's thought that she's likely to get pregnant and need maternity leave	→	A person's gender is not a factor at any stage of the selection process

But it's also about providing the *same opportunities* to everyone. For example:

Discrimination	→	**Outlawing discrimination in recruitment and selection means that**
A blind applicant applies for a job. The application is rejected because the employer assumes the applicant won't be able to do the job	→	The employer and applicant discuss adjustments which could be made to enable the applicant to do the job, e.g. screen reader software, a personal reader, extra lighting

There are two main types of discrimination which equal opportunities laws prevent:

- **direct discrimination**. This involves treating a person less favourably because of their gender, race or because they have a disability
- **indirect discrimination**. This is when a requirement or condition, either intentionally or unintentionally discriminates against males or females, a particular racial group or groups of people with disabilities. For example, if a post advertises that a job is 'full-time' the employer must be able to justify the requirement of 'full-time' as generally fewer women than men can work full-time due to child care commitments.

In some circumstances an employer can specify what sex or race can apply for a particular post. This is called a Genuine Occupational Qualification (GOQ). For example, under the Sex Discrimination Act 1975, a GOQ can be claimed for reasons of physiology (e.g. a job as a model).

Positive discrimination is unlawful. For example, you cannot decide that as women are under-represented at a particular grade, you will only shortlist women and therefore ignore male applicants. However *positive action* can be taken. This involves taking action to create a more even playing field so that under-represented groups can compete equally in the recruitment and selection process. For example:

Specific action points in Arts Council England HR policy

- Arts Council England will ensure that it is able to attract a wide pool of talented candidates from diverse groups and communities, e.g. through advertisements for vacancies placed within media appropriate to the target groups
- we will provide training for interview panels in understanding cultural differences in presentation style and interviewing by job applicants
- we will 'equality-proof' recruitment and selection process, e.g. ensuring that person specifications do not include unnecessary requirements
- we will launch an organization-wide positive action programme, aimed at the under-represented target groups
- we will facilitate the creation and maintenance of dedicated staff networks, covering ethnic minority groups, staff with disabilities, carers, etc.
- we will provide pre-interview training and preparation for staff in under-represented groups seeking promotion to develop presentational skills
- we will make reasonable adjustments in relation to employment so that policies and practices do not discriminate against under-represented groups
- we will encourage job applications from the target groups and operate within appropriate positive action schemes, e.g. guaranteed interview schemes for people with disabilities, pre-employment training for all staff, etc.

(Source: *www.artscouncil.org.uk*, September, 2004)

ACTIVITY 7

Consider the following scenarios. For each one ask yourself:

- Which UK legislation is the discrimination covered by?
- Is it direct or indirect discrimination?

1 *Whilst being interviewed, a job applicant says that she has a same sex partner. Although she has all the skills and competences required of the job holder, the organization decides not to offer her the job because she is a lesbian.*

Legislation:
Type of discrimination:

2 *An advertisement for a job is only put into a particular religious magazine. There is no religious requirement associated with the job requirements.*

Legislation:
Type of discrimination:

3 *An applicant who is deaf and uses sign language has a pre-arranged interview. Communication is difficult as no sign language interpreter at the meeting has been booked for the meeting.*

Legislation:
Type of discrimination:

FEEDBACK

The first scenario is ***direct discrimination*** and is covered by the regulations resulting from the European Directive 2000 (Sexual Orientation) regulations. The second scenario, in the job advertisement, is an example of ***indirect discrimination*** as it is unlikely to be seen by people of other religious beliefs. It would be covered by the European Directive 2000 (Religion or Belief) regulations. The last scenario is ***direct discrimination*** under the Disability Discrimination Act, 1975.

FROM EQUALITY OF OPPORTUNITY TO VALUING DIVERSITY

Promoting equality of opportunity has centred on laws outlawing discrimination. But even with legislation, discrimination is still common. For example:

- The unemployment rate for disabled people is nearly twice that of other people of working age even though 44 per cent of adjustments cost less than £50 (DfES's Good Practice Guide, Age diversity in employment)
- On average women take home 80 per cent of the hourly pay of men.

Valuing diversity involves a more positive approach and results in greater business benefits. It's about organizations *welcoming* the full range of diverse characteristics of people and *wanting* to reflect that diversity in:

1. their workforce (i.e. making sure their employees represent the diversity in the communities they work in)
2. the services provided to customers (i.e. making sure services reflect the diverse needs of people).

Major differences between 'equal opportunities' approaches and 'management of diversity'

Aspect	Equal opportunities	Managing diversity
Case argued	Reduce discrimination	Utilize employee potential to maximum advantage
Whose responsibility	HR/personnel department	All managers
Focuses on	Groups	Individuals
Perspective	Dealing with different needs of different groups	Integrated
Benefit for employees	Opportunities improved for disadvantaged groups, primarily through setting targets	Opportunities improved for all employees
Focus on management activity	Recruitment	Managing
Remedies	Changing systems and practices	Changing the culture

Source: Torrington, D., Hall, L. and Taylor, S. (2002) *Human Resource Management*, Financial Times, Prentice Hall, pp. 371.

A benchmarking programme by the CSR Europe[4] – a network of organizations helping companies to achieve profitability by placing Corporate Social Responsibility into mainstream practice – identifies five main levels on a continuum from 'compliance' with legislation to being 'leaders in diversity'.

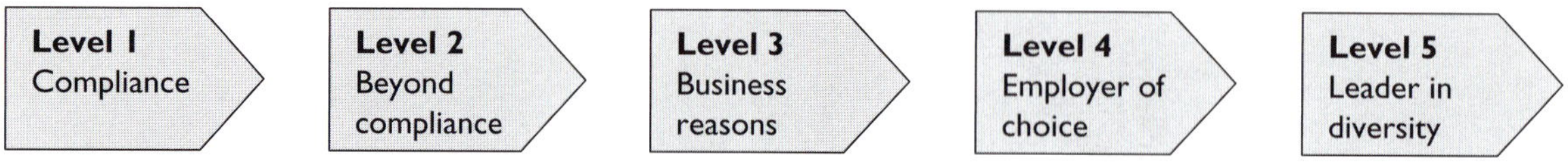

Level 1 Compliance	Level 2 Beyond compliance	Level 3 Business reasons	Level 4 Employer of choice	Level 5 Leader in diversity

Level 1: Compliance
These organizations aim to meet legal obligations. Their focus is on equality (treating everyone in the same way) rather than on diversity (respecting people's differences).

Level 2: Beyond compliance
These organizations go beyond simple compliance by aiming to support historically disadvantaged groups. They are likely to have one or more diversity initiatives in place, but these are isolated and can quickly stop if interest in driving the initiative is lost.

Level 3: Business reasons
These organizations understand that certain diversity initiatives can improve organizational efficiency, recruitment, employee retention, etc. They evaluate diversity initiatives quantitatively and qualitatively. Diversity is seen as a means to an end.

Level 4: Employer of choice
These organizations have internalized diversity as a core organizational value. It's viewed as an essential element of continued growth. Diversity is integrated into all aspects of the organization and all employees consider themselves responsible for creating an environment which is fair and equitable for all.

Level 5: Leader in diversity
These organizations have achieved their internal vision of equity for all and now seek to foster diversity beyond their own boundaries.

Source: Adapted from Section 4 – *The Benchmarking Programme*, Business and Diversity Report, CSR Europe www.csreurope.org

ACTIVITY 8

Consider your organization.

- Is it managing diversity or trying to provide equality of opportunity?

- Where would you place it on the CSR Europe continuum?

FEEDBACK

Many organizations are only beginning to understand the concept of diversity and integrate it into their strategies. You may find it useful discussing the concept with your line manager and Human Resources or Personnel department to find out their perspective.

The remainder of the workbook focuses on the recruitment and selection process and stressing the importance of viewing the process in the context of:

- your organization's policies and procedures
- laws relating to equality of opportunity and employment.

Learning summary

- Diversity is about recognizing and valuing that people are different from each other and adapting workplace practices accordingly. It isn't just about race or gender.
- There is a strong business ethos for diversity which includes better recruitment, increased retention, improved understanding of markets and communities, an enhanced reputation and cost savings.
- Achieving a diverse workforce requires:
  - an organizational strategy
  - individual managers to have a mindset which actively values diversity.
- Equal opportunities legislation is a response to social recognition that:
  1. there is discrimination in society, and
  2. it is unacceptable
- There are two main types of discrimination which equal opportunities laws prevent:
  - **direct discrimination**. This involves treating a person less favourably because of their gender, race or because they have a disability.
  - **indirect discrimination**. This is when a requirement or condition, either intentionally or unintentionally, discriminates against males or females, a particular racial group or groups of people with disabilities.
- Positive discrimination is unlawful; positive action can be taken.
- There has been a considerable shift in attitudes and practices in recent years from compliance with equal opportunity legislation to embracing diversity at work.

Into the workplace

You need to:

- recognize the degree of commitment to diversity in your organization
- check your attitudes towards valuing diversity
- consider the advantages of a diverse workforce to your team and your organization
- understand the main purpose of equal opportunities legislation in the recruitment and selection process.

References

1 Thomas, R.R. (1992) *Beyond Race and Gender: Unleasing the Power of your Total Work Force by Managing Diversity*, Amacon.

2 Adapted from Banks, J. Dividends of Diversity, *Management Focus Issue 12, Summer 1999*, Cranfield School of Management.

3 The Business of Diversity – How Organisations in the Public and Private Sectors are Integrating Equality and Diversity to Enhance Business Performance, 2002, Schneider-Ross, www.Schneider-Ross.com

4 Business and Diversity: Helping Businesses Score Higher in Managing Diversity, a Report by CSR Europe. Http://www.csreurope.org/upload store/cms/docs/CSRE_ pub_diversityDec2002. pdf

Adams, D. (1995) *Hitchhikers Guide to the Galaxy*, Ballantine Books.

Section 2 Selection methods

Introduction

Selecting the best applicant for a job isn't an exact science. Most recruitment and selection processes involve:

- applicants completing an application
- interviews.

It's generally seen as a cost-effective approach. However, it does have its drawbacks and there are other selection methods which *may* be appropriate for you to use.

There are a number of factors to consider when choosing selection methods. For example:

1. Selection criteria for the post to be filled – the limitations of what can accurately be assessed by different selection methods has to be recognized, e.g. the most reliable way of assessing if a person is good at making presentations is to see them deliver one
2. Acceptability and appropriateness of methods – selection methods should be seen as being sensible and meaningful by applicants, e.g. lengthy application forms asking for seemingly irrelevant information may put off applicants from applying
3. Abilities of staff involved in the selection process, e.g. only appropriately qualified people can administer psychological tests
4. Administrative ease – generally the simpler the selection process, the easier it is arrange
5. Time factors – individual interviews can usually be arranged at relatively short notice; tests and assessment centres need to be arranged well in advance
6. Accuracy – selection methods vary in their reliability

(Continued)

7 Cost – decisions have to be made as to whether the cost of tests and assessment centre activities can be justified. Generally, the more senior the post the greater the impact of making a good or bad selection decision. Therefore, higher recruitment costs can often be justified for more senior posts.

Source: Based on Torrington, D., Hall, L., Taylor, S. (2002) *Human Resource Management*, Financial Times Prentice Hall, p. 193.

In this section we look briefly at the most common selection methods:

- applications
- interviews
- work-related tests
- psychological tests
- assessment centres.

Applications

The two main methods for applying are:

- to use a standard form which applicants complete, and/or
- applicants send a curriculum vitae (CV) and a covering letter.

A standard form has three main advantages:

- Replies are easier to assess against the person specification
- Direct comparison of applicants is easier
- Specific questions can focus on what you want to find out.

If you are designing an application form you must take care that all the questions are relevant to deciding if the applicant could meet the person specification criteria. For example, asking questions about marital status or nationality are potentially discriminatory and illegal.

A CV and covering letter enable applicants to express themselves more freely and present themselves creatively. However, it is much more difficult, and time-consuming, to compare applicants against the person specification.

USING APPLICATIONS TO ASSESS BEHAVIOURAL COMPETENCES

The main purpose of applications has traditionally been to collect factual information about an applicant's background and experience. In recent years applications are being used more to assess against person specification. For example:

It was decided that a key requirement of a senior manager post is the ability to '**show a commitment to providing a service**'. Indicators of a person's ability to provide a service were identified as:

- displays honesty and integrity
- shows determination to provide a quality service
- willingness to follow up and through to ensure satisfactory outcomes
- able to design, manage and deliver services to meet customers' requirements
- deals constructively with conflict.

Applicants were asked to provide evidence of their ability to deliver an effective service to meet customers' needs in their initial application.

A typical response from an applicant could have been:

Commitment to providing a service: Management of dredging operations at Weighton My current responsibilities include managing the dredging at the port of Weighton. The estuarial port is situated on the River Kear which has a dynamic regime and requires constant dredging to ensure a commercial schedule can be maintained by three vessels. All dredging is done by contractors and in order to keep costs down a considerable amount of negotiating and organizational skill is required. I plan and optimize work for each campaign. In order to ensure contractors are prepared to return for more work, honesty and integrity in negotiation are essential. To ensure value for money and maintain depths, constant monitoring and input is required for each campaign to ensure satisfactory outcomes. I need to deal with the constant conflict between the commercial requirements of the service and the safety of navigation to ensure the latter prevails with minimum detriment to the former.

USE OF BIODATA AT THE APPLICATION STAGE

The use of biodata can trace its origins to the 1920s when personal characteristics of 'good' 'middling' and 'poor' salesmen were identified. Information was then collected from applicants for the post of salesmen and compared with characteristics of existing salesmen to predict performance in the job.

The same principle is still used although techniques have evolved. Typical questions might include:

- How many hours in a typical week do you watch television?
  (i) none; (ii) up to 3 hours; (iii) 3–7 hours; (iv) 7–12 hours; (v) over 12 hours
- How many brothers and sisters do you have?
  (i) none; (ii) one; (iii) two; (iv) three; (v) four; (vi) five

Commonly, biodata is collected through the applicant answering a series of multiple choice questions at the application stage and is used to sift through a large number of applications. It involves high development costs.

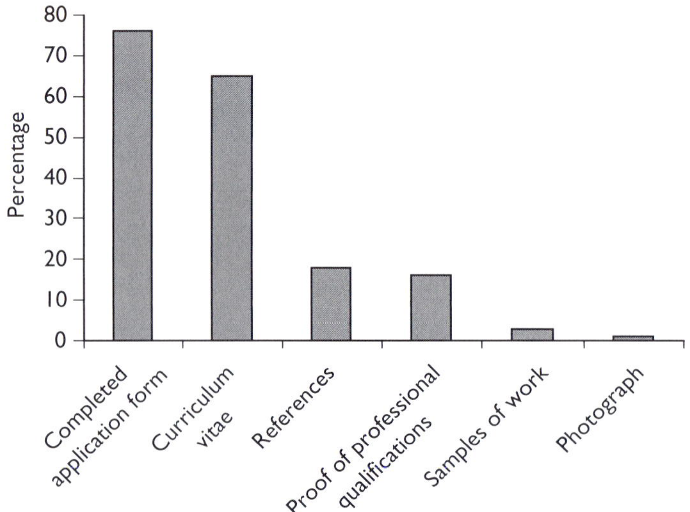

Figure 2.1 What do organizations wish to see in order to select candidates for interview? Adapted from *Managing Best Practice No. 99 Recruitment and Selection* (2002), The Work Foundation: http://www.theworkfoundation.com/servlet/IndSocProduct?id = 13551515X

Interviews

Interviews vary widely from brief one-to-one meetings to a succession of panel interviews. Usually the seniority of the post dictates:

- the number of interviews during the selection process
- who does the interviewing
- how many interviewers.

- Eighteen per cent or organizations always use one-to-one interviews; 41 per cent sometimes use them, 40 per cent never
- When using panel interviews, 51 per cent of organizations use two to three people
- Thirty-four per cent of organizations try to achieve a gender balance on interview panels; 20 per cent try to achieve a race balance

Source: Managing Best Practice No. 99 Recruitment and Selection (2002), The Work Foundation: http://www.theworkfoundation.com/servlet/IndSocProduct?id = 13551515X

ACTIVITY 9

What advantages are there of a panel interview?

FEEDBACK

Research has shown that two or more interviewers give more reliable results than one-to-one interviews. This may be due to greater emphasis on planning or opportunity for note-taking or that less prejudice creeps in as decisions have to be justified amongst panel members. Equal opportunities bodies recommend the use of panels in preference to one-to-one interviews. However, panels should be kept small. Too many people can be intimidating and ask disjointed questions.

Interviews have a relatively poor record of validity (i.e. how well they assess a candidate's ability to do a job). Reasons include:

- The competence of the interviewers, e.g. Research[1] has shown that interviewers accept or reject a candidate within the first three or four minutes of the interview and spend the rest of the time looking for evidence to confirm their initial impression.
- The motivation of the interviewers to remain focused. Concentration has been shown to wander towards the end of interviewing for a day; interviewers have also been shown to stay more focused if they know they have to justify their decision to someone after the interview.
- Whether or not the candidate has received interview coaching. Research[2] has shown that people who have been trained do perform better at interviews.
- Whether or not the candidate lies.

HOW RELIABLE ARE INTERVIEWS?

Research[3] has shown that candidates do not perform consistently at different interviews. There was more agreement between interviewers who attended the same interview (0.77), than between interviewers who attended different interviews with the same candidate (0.53). Interviews were more reliable if based on job analysis and if the interviewers were trained.

We look in detail at the skills of conducting an interview, and increasing reliability, in Section 4.

Work-related tests

There may be some key skills which are critical to job success. These skills can often be tested by work-related tests during the interview process. For example:

- skills tests or tests of physical ability
- cognitive tests, e.g. literacy, numeracy
- work simulations, e.g. word processing, making a presentation, in-tray exercises.

If you set up a test, make sure that you clearly identify the criteria against which the candidates will be assessed.

ACTIVITY 10

What criteria might you use to assess candidates who had been asked to prepare and deliver a five-minute presentation during the selection process. For example, your criteria may include:

- Does the candidate engage the audience?
- Does the candidate present information clearly and accurately?

Make a note of three more criteria.

1

2

3

FEEDBACK

It's essential that you identify *exactly* what criteria you're assessing candidates against in any work-related tests. Spending time identifying the relevant criteria will ensure that you get an accurate, reliable result and that the test is fair for all candidates.

Psychological tests

The Chartered Institute of Personnel and Development (CIPD) define psychological tests as:

'tests which can be systematically scored and administered, which are used to measure individual differences (for example, in personality, aptitude, ability, attainment or intelligence). They are supported by a body of evidence and statistical data which demonstrates their validity and are used in an occupational setting'

These tests should only be carried out by people who are fully trained in their use and interpretation. Used appropriately, they have been shown to enhance the decision-making process in the selection process.

The word 'test' is misleading. For example, some tests look at personality traits and give a feel for a candidate's strengths and personality profile. Generally they try to give indications as to:

1. Does the candidate have the right personality?
2. Will she or he be able to do the job?
3. How will she or he behave at work?
4. Does the applicant have any problems that will interfere with work?

Respondents were asked whether their organizations use psychometric testing when assessing candidates.

- Fifty-four per cent of respondents' organizations do use psychometric testing/profiles when assessing; 42 per cent do not
- Only 3 per cent plan to introduce this assessment method in the next three months.

Of those respondents whose organizations do use psychometric testing profiles when assessing candidates:

- more than two-thirds of these organizations (64%) buy their psychometric tests 'off-the-shelf' and only 5 per cent design them in-house
- almost one-third (30%) of these respondents use tests produced by external consultants.

Managing Best Practice No. 99 Recruitment and Selection (2002), The Work Foundation: http://www.theworkfoundation.com/servlet/IndSocProduct?id = 13551515X.

ACTIVITY 11

The website www.shldirect.com (Saville and Holdsworth) offers practice tests designed for candidates. You may find it useful too if you are considering using psychological testing in your selection process.

FEEDBACK

CIPD recommend that before selecting a test an employer should receive satisfactory answers from the test suppliers to the following questions:

- How reliable is the test and how consistent is it as a measure?
- How valid is the test and does it really identify the attributes or skills which the supplier claims?
- What evidence can suppliers provide that their tests do not unfairly disadvantage certain groups?
- Will the test seem appropriate in the eyes of those taking it and what have previous reactions been to this test?
- Has the test been used effectively in similar circumstances?
- Are the norms provided by the supplier for comparative purposes up-to-date and appropriate for the user's requirements? Do the norm results apply to a sufficiently representative mix of occupations, gender or ethnic groups to allow fair comparison with the user's group?
- Is the method of test evaluation and scoring appropriate to the purpose for which the test will be used?

Psychometric testing

There may be gender differences in how men and women answer certain personality questionnaires. In the article *Psychometrics Should Make Assessment Fairer (Equal Opportunities Review 67)* Robert Wood notes that there is some recent evidence that, on the OPQ at any rate (the most widely-used questionnaire in this country), some gender-related differences may show up. Specifically, it appears that the propensity of males to puff themselves up more than females results in differences opening up on scales like "persuasive", "innovative" and "controlling". If those relying on the results of such questionnaires do not take account of this, indirect sex discrimination could result.

www.eoc-law.org.uk (September 2004)

Assessment centres

An 'assessment centre' is the term used for giving candidates a number of exercises and activities (work-based tests, group activities, psychological tests, individual interviews). The assessment centre may last from half a day to two days, and typically would involve up to 12 candidates.

Throughout the assessment centre the candidates would be assessed by a number of trained observers. At the end of the assessment centre the observers meet to pool their scores and decide on the most appropriate applicant(s). Some assessment centres result in a short-list being produced for final interview.

Assessment centres may be:

- designed by your organization (often involving people from the recruitment and selection department as well as the line manager)
- bought 'off-the-shelf' from recruitment consultants
- tailor-made and run by recruitment consultants.

Assessment centres are expensive to run and usually only used for senior posts.

ACTIVITY 12

What selection methods have you had experience of?

As an employer:	**As a candidate:**

Which do you think are the most appropriate selection methods to appoint members of your team? Consider your own experience as a candidate and refer to the list of factors to consider at the start of the section.

FEEDBACK

You may have concluded that different selection methods to the ones you are currently using might be appropriate. If so, you may find it helpful to discuss your response with members of your Human Resource or Personnel department.

Learning summary

- Methods of selection include:
  - applications
  - interviews
  - work-related tests
  - psychological tests
  - assessment centres.
- Completing an application followed by an interview is the most common method of selection
- Factors to consider when choosing selection methods include:
  - Selection criteria for the post to be filled
  - Acceptability and appropriateness of methods
  - Abilities of staff involved in the selection
  - Administrative ease
  - Time factors
  - Accuracy of selection methods
  - Cost.

Into the workplace

You need to:

- identify the selection methods which are most appropriate to the appointment of members of your team.

References

1 Webster, E.C. (1964) *Decision-making in the Employment Interview*, Toronto Industrial Relations Centre, McGill University, Canada

2 Maurer, T.J., Solamon, J.M. and Troxtel, D.D. (1998) Relations of coaching with performance in situational employment interviews, *Journal of Applied Psychology*, 83, 128–136

3 Conway, J.M., Jako, R.A. and Googman, D.F. (1995) A meta-analysis of inter-rater and internal consistency reliability of selection interviews, *Journal of Applied Psychology*, 80, 565–579

Section 3 Focusing on recruitment

Introduction

Recruitment is the part of the process which starts with deciding if there is a vacancy to be filled and ends with receiving applications. It involves:

1. Deciding if there is a vacancy to be filled
2. Writing a job description
3. Writing a person specification
4. Deciding on the selection process
5. Attracting applicants
6. Managing the response.

In this section, we look at each of these steps. As you work through the section you need to put the context of the section within the policies and procedures of your own organization.

Recruitment within the context of your organization

The policies and procedures of your organization will set the framework for how you handle recruitment. In some organizations managers are responsible for the recruitment and selection process; in others the Human Resource or Personnel department take control of the process with input from managers where necessary.

ACTIVITY 13

Contact the department or person who deals with recruitment within the Personnel or Human Resources department in your organization. Find out:

- What are their expectations of managers in the recruitment and selection process?
- What role do they play in the recruitment and selection process?

In which, if any, of the following areas do the Personnel or Human Resources department offer you, as a manager, support?

- Writing a job description
- Writing a person specification
- Deciding on the selection process
- Attracting applicants (advertising, sending out application forms and information)
- Managing the response (i.e. administrative help in dealing with returned applications)
- Running or supporting the selection process (e.g. interviews, assessment centres)
- What policies and procedures are relevant to recruitment and selection? If so, what are they?
- Is there any in-house recruitment and selection training for managers?
- Who can you contact if you have questions about recruitment and selection?
- Does the organization have a human resource strategy? If so, what is it?

FEEDBACK

It's essential that you use your organization's policies and procedures as the framework for the way in which you recruit and select. The remaining sections of the workbook give an insight into the practicalities involved.

Is there a vacancy to be filled?

A potential vacancy gives you an opportunity to review requirements and check whether:

- it is a straight-forward replacement
- a different job needs to be advertised
- the work can be covered by other means.

You need to be open-minded, creative and explore options. For example, could you:

- Reallocate work? A reorganization of responsibilities within existing staff may give development opportunities or simply be sensible
- Contract out all or part of the work? Many organizations are assessing the costs of employing people against the costs of contracting out the work. Is using agency staff an option?
- Cover the responsibilities by introducing more flexible working hours for existing staff?
- Use an internal secondment?
- Upgrade software and train existing staff?

What's important is that you rigorously question the need to fill a vacancy and the nature of the vacancy.

Write a job description

Once you've decided that there is a vacancy to fill, the next step is to write a job description which sets out clearly the main responsibilities of the post. It's very important that it is clear and describes the job accurately as it:

- communicates to applicants what the job involves
- ensures that everyone involved in the recruitment process is clear about what the job involves
- lays the foundation for getting the right person to do the job.

Before you write a job description it's often useful to:

1 analyse the job
2 analyse what's happening in the organization.

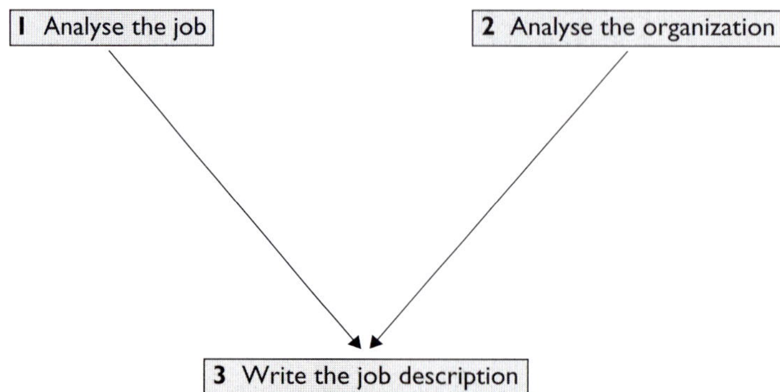

ANALYSING THE JOB

Many jobs evolve over time and outgrow the role which existed when the jobholder began.

An analysis of a job involves identifying what the current job entails in terms of:

- its purpose
- responsibilities, including approximate percentage of time
- decision-making authority
- quantitative measures relating to the job
- job related knowledge and skills.

Analysis involves standing back and trying to capture all the dimensions of the job before you consider the job description. The existing jobholder can often be a good source of information as they'll have the most knowledge about what the current job involves.

For example (see opposite)

Job analysis: Corporate Recruitment Assistant		
Purpose: To provide recruitment advice and assistance to line managers		
Responsibilities:	**Includes:**	**Time (%)**
1 Supporting line managers with recruitment and selection process	■ Identifying improvements to job descriptions and person specifications ■ Placing adverts in external press ■ Providing advice to line managers ■ Giving feedback to candidates ■ Sending out application packs	75
2 Data processing	■ Generating HR data ■ Monitoring equal opportunities data	20
3 Training	■ Assisting with recruitment and selection training course ■ Coaching new members of team	10
Decision-making authority: Approving external adverts, providing legislative advice to managers		
Quantitative measures: Answering approximately 80 queries from managers a week; Approving 20 external adverts		
Job-related knowledge and skills: ■ CIPD graduate qualification ■ Experience of working within high volume recruitment service ■ Knowledge of recruitment legislation ■ Has good communication skills ■ Ability to explain policies and procedures to managers ■ Use of word processing and database systems ■ Ability to interpret statistical data ■ Ability to proofread documents		

Once you have captured what the current job involves you need to consider what's happening in the wider organization.

ANALYSING THE ORGANIZATION

This involves answering the question, 'Do the plans for the organization have any impact on this job role?' You may be involved in developing service or business plans for your department, in which case you will be aware of future plans. If not, you may need to talk to your line manager.

WRITING THE JOB DESCRIPTION

Once you have analysed the job and considered organizational developments you can move on to writing the job description. Ask yourself the question 'What will I want this person to do:

- now?
- to meet any changes in the foreseeable future?

For example, supposing you are currently recruiting an administrative assistant who has no contact with the customers but you know there are plans to change the role so this person will be in direct contact with customers. It would be sensible to include reference to the new responsibility in the job description so that applicants know and so that you can reflect the new responsibility within the person specification.

A job description is an outline of the main responsibilities to be performed by the job holder. Your organization may have a standard format for writing job descriptions. If so, it is likely to include:

- The job title
- The main purpose of the job. This should be a single sentence which describes why the role exists
- The main tasks of the job – these should start with active verbs and be as precise as possible.

For example:

❑ Administer	❑ Operate
❑ Analyze	❑ Organize
❑ Approve	❑ Participate
❑ Budget	❑ Prepare
❑ Carry out	❑ Process
❑ Compile	❑ Produce
❑ Comply	❑ Propose
❑ Consult	❑ Provide
❑ Co-ordinate	❑ Respond
❑ Deal with	❑ Represent
❑ Design	❑ Review
❑ Develop	❑ Select
❑ Evaluate	❑ Set
❑ Forecast	❑ Structure
❑ Give	❑ Supervise
❑ Identify	❑ Support
❑ Implement	❑ Take
❑ Inspect	❑ Train
❑ Lead	❑ Undertake
❑ Maintain	❑ Uphold
❑ Manage	❑ Use
❑ Monitor	❑ Verify
❑ Motivate	

Reference to a job analysis can be particularly useful as it will help you to extract the main tasks of the post:

- Who the job holder is responsible to
- Who the job holder is responsible for (if applicable)
- Any special conditions
- Date the job description was written or updated.

For example:

Job title: Corporate Recruitment Assistant

Purpose: To provide recruitment advice and assistance to line managers

Reporting to: Corporate Recruitment Manager

Main responsibilities:

- Respond to enquiries relating to recruitment and selection from line managers
- Support line managers to write job descriptions, person specifications and job advertisements
- Deal with local and national press when placing job advertisements
- Compile and send out recruitment packs
- Manage application response
- Maintain database and generate information

Alternatively a job description may focus on key results areas. For example:

Job title:	Corporate Training Manager
Department:	Human Resources
Location:	Birmingham
Hours:	36 hours per week
Responsible to:	Human Resource Director
Responsible for:	Corporate Training Assistant
Purpose of job:	To implement a strategic approach to meeting the corporate training and development

(Continued)

Key results areas
1 Implementation of corporate initiatives
1.1 To develop resources and networks to implement corporate initiatives which involve changes in employees' skills, knowledge or behaviours 1.2 To monitor and evaluate the implementation of the training elements of corporate initiatives
2 Liaison, networking and information
2.1 To liaise regularly with divisional training officers 2.2 To ensure regular exchanges of information and to keep an accessible central store of the information 2.3 To network with cross divisional forums to offer support and expertise in aspects of training and development

ACTIVITY 14

Review your own job description and the ones of people in your team. Are they accurate reflections of the work you do? If not, update them by following the process outlined above. Make sure that you follow any in-house style for writing job descriptions.

FEEDBACK

It's important that job descriptions are kept up-to-date. Outside the recruitment and selection process, job descriptions can be used:

- during induction
- in appraisal meetings
- to identify development needs
- in restructuring activities
- in job evaluation projects.

Preparing a person specification

A person specification sets out the skills, knowledge and experience needed to do the job. It's very important within the recruitment process as it:

- Clarifies exactly what you are looking for in a person
- Communicates to potential applicants what you are looking for
- Allows you to compare applicants against pre-set criteria
- Provides a structure for interview and main areas of questioning
- Helps you to be objective
- Ensures the selection process is fair and transparent.

Each item on a person specification must be justified by the job description. For example, in the job description for a Corporate Recruitment Assistant, one of the responsibilities is 'respond to enquiries'. Therefore, you'd expect reference to communication skills to be part of the person specification. The role also includes using databases. Therefore, reference to computer skills would also be expected in the person specification.

Job descriptions/person specifications

'Check that these include only requirements related to the duties. A good discipline is to focus on what the job is to accomplish – the inclusion of unnecessary or marginal requirements in a job specification can lead to discrimination.'

Source: *Employing disabled people: a good practice guide for managers and employers* (DfEE)

PRACTICALITIES OF WRITING A PERSON SPECIFICATION

As with job descriptions, your organization may have a standard format for preparing job descriptions. A typical person specification would include:

- Skills and abilities such as word processing skills, administrative abilities, managerial skills
- Qualifications, e.g. are any professional qualifications essential or desirable? Are practical or vocational qualifications a minimum requirement e.g. food hygiene certificate
- Knowledge, e.g. knowledge of a particular industry, knowledge of a particular aspect of the public sector
- Experience. This may involve considering the minimum work experience required of the job holder. Alternatively, experience from non-paid activities may be equally valid.
- Special conditions. This includes anything specific that the jobholder would have to do, e.g. wear a uniform, work unsocial hours, live-in at weekends.

For example, a person specification for the role of Corporate Training Manager may include:

Person specification: Corporate Training Manager

1 Knowledge

1.1 Understanding of current good practice in organizational training and development

1.2 Knowledge of customer-focused and needs-led service delivery

1.3 MIPD qualified

2 Skills/abilities

2.1 Able to use a range of consultation methods to research and identify customer needs

2.2 Able to build relationships with senior managers

2.3 Able to make formal presentations

2.4 Able to develop creative approaches to the development and evaluation of training initiatives

3 Experience (essential)

3.1 Experience of developing a training strategy

3.2 Experience of leading teams to develop a range of cost effective training solutions

Some person specifications also highlight which criteria are essential and which are seen as being desirable.

When you write a person specification take care that:

- anything that is classed as essential should refer to minimum requirements
- the person specification isn't too long.

Therefore, keep to a minimum. If you overstate what is required, you run the risk of losing good applicants and being discriminatory. For example, specifying educational qualifications such as 'A' levels, often tells you little about what a person can do in the workplace but discriminate against some people whose educational pathway was disrupted due to disability such as being blind or partially sighted.

You need to assess against each of the criteria and applicants can find over-long person specifications off-putting. It's often easy to double-up on criteria and have similar criteria appearing under both skills and knowledge.

ACTIVITY 15

Select an updated job description for a member on your team. Write a person specification for it. Again, make sure you follow any in-house style.

FEEDBACK

Ask for feedback on the person specification from either your line manager or personnel department. You are likely to find that it takes a number of drafts before it accurately reflects the requirements of the post.

THE IMPORTANCE OF MANAGING EXPECTATIONS

It's easy to fall into the trap of demanding too much in a person specification. It can lead to appointing people who are over-qualified for the post. If this results in them feeling let down and dissatisfied they are likely to leave at the earliest opportunity – and you're left with having to recruit all over again.

'False impressions are given and a positive spin put on answers to questions so as to deter able applicants from taking up alternative offers. As a result, graduates start work confident in the belief that their days will be filled with interesting work, that they will be treated fairly and objectively in terms of performance assessment, that their career development will be fostered judiciously and that their working lives will in some way be 'fun' and 'exciting'. That is fine if it really can be guaranteed. Unfortunately, such is not the case, and unsurprisingly it leads to early dissatisfaction and higher turnover rates than are desirable.'

Source: Jenner, S. and Taylor, S. (2000) *Recruiting, Developing and Retaining Graduate Talent*, Financial Times, Prentice Hall, p.155

Choosing selection methods

Section 2 explored some of the main selection methods available. Whatever methods you use, always bear in mind the person specification when you choose selection methods. You should be able to identify when you are going to assess each criteria listed.

For example:

Person specification:		Corporate Training Manager
1	**Knowledge**	**Where will it be assessed?**
1.1	Understanding of current good practice in organizational training and development	Specialist interview during assessment centre
1.2	Knowledge of customer-focused and needs-led service delivery	Specialist interview during assessment centre
1.3	MIPD qualified	Application form
2	**Skills/abilities**	
2.1	Able to use a range of consultation methods to research and identify customer needs	Group activity during assessment centre
2.2	Able to build relationships with senior managers	Group activity during assessment centre/specialist interview
2.3	Able to make formal presentations	Assessment centre activity
2.4	Able to develop creative approaches to the development and evaluation of training initiatives	Specialist interview during assessment centre

If you are simply using an application form followed by an interview, make sure that questions during the interview explore all the criteria listed in the person specification. Criteria on the person specification should never be ignored during the selection process.

Attracting applicants

An initial decision has to be made over whether the vacancy will be advertised internally or externally.

ACTIVITY 16

What are the advantages of filling a vacancy internally?

FEEDBACK

The knowledge that it's common practice to fill vacancies internally:

- is motivating for existing employees as they know there is progression within the organization
- is often more reliable, you know the person
- tends to be cheaper.

However, recruiting internally may be missing an opportunity to increase diversity and bring fresh ideas into the organization. Some organization's have policies to always recruit externally.

PLACING AN ADVERT

The main aim of advertising a vacancy is to attract applicants who can meet the person specification; the emphasis has to be on quality rather than quantity. You don't want to waste time having to review application forms from people who wouldn't be able to do the job.

If your organization has a house-style for advertisements you must follow it, e.g. include correctly positioned logo. Many organizations also include an equal opportunities statement on advertisements.

Advertisements should include:

- job title
- location
- brief description of the job

- brief description of the organization
- indication of experience required
- instructions for reply and closing date – it is good practice to include the date of any assessment centre.

Always make sure you proofread advertisements; mistakes can easily creep in. You also need to check that they don't contravene equal opportunities legislation.

Equal Opportunities Commission v Eldridge McFarlane-Watts [1990] IT, unreported

The respondent, a firm of solicitors in Oxford, advertised in the Oxford Times for a secretary. The advertisement made it clear that a female secretary was being sought. The advertisement came to the notice of the EOC, which wrote to both the respondent and the Oxford Times advising them that the advertisement might be unlawful. The solicitors replied that if the advertisement breached the SDA they very much regretted this, as it was completely unintentional.

The newspaper stated that although it had a system of vetting advertisements, this particular advertisement appeared to have slipped through, perhaps because it was written in a light-hearted vein and was placed by solicitors whom it would have expected to know the law. The newspaper apologized for having breached the Act.

The EOC issued proceedings against the solicitors firm claiming that the advertisement indicated or might reasonably be understood as indicating an intention to recruit a woman for the job and that the advertisement was therefore in breach of s38 (1) of the SDA.

The respondent did not appear at the hearing, but sent in a written submission, claiming that it was not its common practice to refer in advertisements to either men or women and the use of the word 'she' in the advertisement had been a mere oversight. Reading IT found that the advertisement, "with its eye-catching flippancy", was discriminatory within s38.

Source www.eoc.org.uk (September 2004)

By carefully selecting where you advertise you can increase the diversity of applicants. Equal opportunity statements in advertisements can also encourage a wider selection of people to apply.

ACTIVITY 17

Refer to your organization's recruitment policy. What key processes do you have to follow for:

- advertising internally?

- advertising externally?

FEEDBACK

If you draft an advertisement, always get feedback from the HR or Personnel department before finalizing it.

Good practice vacancy advertising

- Wherever possible, all vacancies will be advertised simultaneously internally and externally.
- Steps will be taken to ensure that knowledge of vacancies reaches under-represented groups internally and externally.
- Wherever possible, vacancies will be notified to job centres, careers offices, schools, colleges, polytechnics, etc. with significant minority group roles, as well as to minority press/media and organizations.
- All vacancy advertisements will include an appropriate short statement on equal opportunity.

Source: www.cre.gov.uk (September 2004)

USING THE INTERNET IN RECRUITMENT

In recent years there has been increased use of the Internet in the recruitment process.

- 14.7 per cent of employers use a job board to post their vacancies
- 39 per cent of organizations reported accepting applications by email
- more than 1/3 publish information for candidates on their corporate sites
- 45 per cent of organizations supply application forms in electronic form to be printed off and returned as hard copy
- 3.6 per cent administer selection tests online.

CIPD, Recruitment and Retention, 2003 Survey www.cipd.co.uk/surveys

Organizations often use a combination of advertising on their own website and also using specialist recruitment sites, e.g. Monster and Totaljobs.

ACTIVITY 18

Below is a comparison of the process of traditional printed advertising with Internet recruiting.

	Traditional	Internet
1	A job vacancy is advertised in the press	A job vacancy is advertised on the Internet
2	A job seeker writes or telephones for more details and/or an application form	All the company and job details are on the website together with an online application form
3	A job seeker returns the application form and/or CV by post	A job seeker returns the application form electronically
4	Manager/Personnel review the written application forms or CVs	Specialized computer software reviews the application forms for an initial match with the organization's requirements

Source: www.cipd.co.uk (September 2004)

Identify two advantages and two disadvantages of using the Internet in the recruitment process.

Advantages	**Disadvantages**
1	**1**
2	**2**

FEEDBACK

Advertising, as well as applying on-line, has advantages. It can speed up the process and reduce recruitment costs (e.g. less time spent on sending out information and application forms).

Using your organization's existing website can give prospective applicants an opportunity to learn more about the organization's culture and values which may increase the likelihood that candidates apply when they are best suited. Candidates can also register to receive information on future vacancies. Research[2] has shown that the reasons organizations use e-recruitment include:

- improved employer profile and corporate image (80%)
- reduced recruitment costs (78%)
- reduced administrative burden (62%)
- better tools for recruitment team (62%)
- shorter recruitment cycle (56%)
- expectation/preference of candidates (51%)
- better fit (screening large pool) (33%)
- Pan-European/global recruitment (24%)
- more effective skills deployment internally (18%)
- recruitment difficulties (11%)

However, there are disadvantages. Not everyone has access to the Internet. For many applicants, it is not the preferred method, and not all organizations have the knowledge or senior manager commitment to developing e-recruitment. Research has also shown that there are gender, ethnicity and age issues (Bartrum[2] 2000).

Handling applications and managing the response

There has to be a mechanism in place for handling the response created by advertising the post. You need to:

- Pre-prepare any documentation you plan to send out. For example, in a print-based process this would usually include:
  - job description
  - person specification
  - covering letter
  - some information about your organization
  - application form.
- Make sure you have the people in place to send out the information and deal with any queries which may arise from potential applicants
- Decide how you will acknowledge the applications as you receive them e.g. will you acknowledge each application as it arrives or will you wait and send either an invitation to interview or letter to inform that the application has been unsuccessful?
- Make sure you have a system in place for dealing with returned applications (e.g. who will collect them together? What will happen to them next?)
- Monitor the response so that you can evaluate the success of your chosen process. For example, by keeping a list of the applicants who requested information so that you know what percentage translated into actual applicants.

EQUAL OPPORTUNITIES MONITORING FORM

If your organization has an equal opportunities policy it's likely that an equal opportunities monitoring form will be sent out at this stage as an option for applicants to complete. Monitoring the background of job applicants serves a number of purposes:

- operational grounds – as we saw in Section 1, diversity brings business benefits
- moral grounds – to see if the equal opportunities are being translated into practice
- legal grounds – unfair discrimination, whether direct or indirect, can be challenged by applicants.

Usual information to be collected includes:

- sex
- ethnic origin
- any disabilities
- age.

Some organizations also ask for information related to religion and sexual orientation.

There is no point collecting information unless it is analysed and used. For example, to assess levels of response from black and ethnic minority groups compared with the overall labour force; to analyse if disproportionately high number of either male or female being shortlisted.

It is illegal to use the information as part of the selection process.

ACTIVITY 19

Does your organization monitor equal opportunities during the recruitment process? If so, talk to your HR or Personnel department to find out what happens to the information collected.

FEEDBACK

The case for diversity was put forward in Section 1. Bridging the gap between theory and practice involves relatively simple steps in the recruitment process. For example, some practical advice, given by the Council for Racial Equality (www.cre.org.uk) for increasing the number of ethnic minority staff includes:

- State clearly in all your job advertisements that you are an equal opportunities employer.
- Place job advertisements in ethnic minority newspapers, magazines and websites, whether local or national
- Review all your job advertising, recruitment and selection procedures. Make sure that the person specification for a vacant post truly matches the requirements of the job. Requiring, or favouring, qualifications that are not necessary to do the job competently can exclude able candidates. For instance, giving preference to applicants because they have a university degree, when the vacancy is for a receptionist's post, may deny the job to an applicant whose experience and ability makes them more suitable
- The law only allows an employer to advertise for members of a particular racial group where membership of a particular group is a 'genuine occupational requirement'.

Making sure that your recruitment is not only fair but also encourages diversity needs rigorous examination of all standard practices in the recruitment process.

Learning summary

- It's essential that you use your organization's policies and procedures as the framework for your recruitment and selection activities.
- Recruitment involves:
  1. Deciding if there is a vacancy to be filled
  2. Writing a job description
  3. Writing a person specification
  4. Deciding on the selection process
  5. Attracting applicants
  6. Managing the response.
- Before you write a job description:
  1. Analyse the job
  2. Analyse what's happening in the organization.
- A person specification sets out the skills, knowledge and experience needed to do the job. Each item on a person specification must be justified by the job description.
- By carefully selecting where you advertise you can increase the diversity of applicants.

- Make sure you have a mechanism in place for handling the response created by advertising the post.
- Make sure that your recruitment practices are not only fair but also encourage diversity.

Into the workplace

You need to:

- update job descriptions and person specification for your team
- manage the recruitment process, working with your organization's Human Resource or Personnel department as appropriate.

References

1 IES Survey 2002, www.employment-studies.co.uk

2 Bartrum D (2000) Internal recruitment and selection: kissing frogs to find princes, *International Journal of Selection and Assessment*, 8, 261–274

Section 4 The selection process

Introduction

The selection process begins when you start to assess the applications you've received. It includes:

- creating a shortlist
- assessing the shortlisted candidates
- making a decision
- communicating the outcome.

The success of the selection process is, to a large extent, dependent on the foundations you laid during the recruitment process. As with recruitment, it is essential that all the actions you take follow your organization's policies and procedures.

Creating a shortlist

A shortlist is a list of the candidates who will move into the next stage of the selection process. After sifting through applications, a manageable shortlist is generally up to twelve candidates.

The key to creating a shortlist is to review the applications against the person specification. It needs to be done systematically so that applications are assessed only against criteria in the person specification. If you receive a huge number of applications you may need to first create a 'longlist' of the applicants who meet selected essential criteria. You can then focus on your longlist in more detail in order to draw up the shortlist.

Prepare a form which lists the criteria on the person specification so you can record the strength of each applicant against each criterion. You may decide to use some form of scoring process, e.g. 1 = strongly met, 2 = partly met, 3 = not referred to at all. It may not be sensible to try to assess all the criteria from the application form so there may be certain criteria that you ignore at this stage. For example, *ability to work under pressure.*

Job title:	**Marketing manager**				
Candidate:	A	B	C	D	E
Knowledge (essential)					
Marketing	1	1	1	2	1
Project management	2	1	2	3	1
Knowledge (desirable)					
Market research	1	1	2	3	3
Skills and abilities (essential)					
Planning and scheduling	n/a	n/a	n/a	n/a	n/a
Written communication skills	1	2	1	1	1
Database management	1	1	1	1	1
Work under pressure	n/a	n/a	n/a	n/a	n/a
Presentational skills	n/a	n/a	n/a	n/a	n/a
Lead a team	n/a	n/a	n/a	n/a	n/a

n/a: not assessed

Shortlisting should be carried out by more than one person. It can be done:

- independently, followed by a meeting to agree the final list
- by working together through the applications.

You need to keep documentation relating to shortlisting for up to six months in order to deal with any complaints about discrimination. Not only has the process to be fair, you also have to be able to *prove* that the process was fair.

ACTIVITY 20

What legislation applies at the shortlisting stage of the selection process?

FEEDBACK

Legislation is in place to prevent discrimination on the grounds of race, gender or disability. Unless there is a Genuine Occupational Qualification, a person's race, gender or disability must not influence the shortlisting process.

Selection and recruitment

- Selection criteria (job description and employee specification) will be kept under constant review to ensure that they are justifiable on non-discriminatory grounds as being essential for the effective performance of the job
- Wherever possible, more than one person must be involved in the selection interview and recruitment process, and all should have received training in equal opportunities
- Wherever possible, women, minorities and disabled persons will be involved in the shortlisting and interviewing processes
- Reasons for selection and rejection of applicants for vacancies must be recorded.

Source: www.cre.gov.uk (September 2004)

Assessing the shortlisted candidates – the selection interview

Your work in the recruitment part of the process will already have identified how you will assess the shortlisted candidates.

If you are planning to use a work-related test make sure:

- you are clear about which aspects of the person specification you are testing
- the criteria you are assessing are critical to job success (otherwise there's no point putting the resources into a test)
- you have a clear marking or rating system.
- any psychological tests are only be carried out by people who are fully trained in their use and interpretation.

> **Key point**
>
> The principle of assessing against the criteria on the person specification applies to all assessment methods.

We look in detail at the running of a selection interview.

In a survey conducted some years ago among a dozen top United Kingdom employers,[1] it was discovered that the chances of an employer finding a good employee through the hiring-interview was only 3 per cent better than if they had picked a name out of a hat. In a further ironic finding, it was discovered that if the interview were conducted by someone who would be working directly with the candidate, the success rate dropped to 2 per cent below that of picking a name out of a hat. Finally, if the interviews were conducted by a so-called personnel expert, the success rate dropped to 10 per cent below that of picking a name out of a hat.[2]

WHAT'S HAPPENING IN A SELECTION INTERVIEW?

In an interview, most of the time is spent by:

- you asking questions
- the candidate answering them.

The emphasis has to be on finding out information; you're there to find out if the candidate meets the person specification.

However, a lot more goes on during an interview than the candidate simply answering questions. From the moment the candidate walks in through the door you're both picking up messages about each other. What's important to recognize is that the candidate's performance, and hence the reliability of the interview, will be affected by **how** you conduct the interview. Questions are asked to gather information and also allow the candidates to sell themselves. You want to select the best person for the job; not the person who is the most confident in the interview situation.

Therefore you need to focus on:

- finding out information so that that you can assess if the candidate meets the person specification, and
- putting the candidate at ease so they can give their best performance.

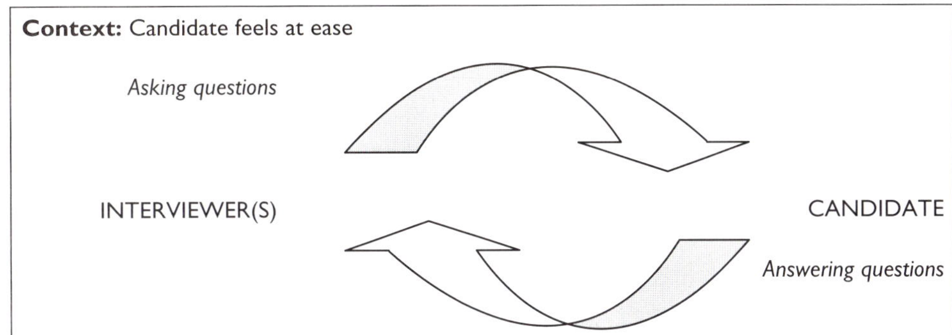

Figure 4.1 The selection interview

As an interviewer you need to be skilled at finding out information and creating an atmosphere which brings out the best in candidates. The two skills are inextricably linked and involve:

- carefully preparing for the interview process
- reviewing how you communicate with people and the impression you give.

PREPARING FOR THE INTERVIEW

You need to:

- prepare questions
- plan the structure of the interview
- prepare the room
- check administrative details.

Prepare questions

To help you prepare questions you should refer to the person specification and the application form from each candidate.

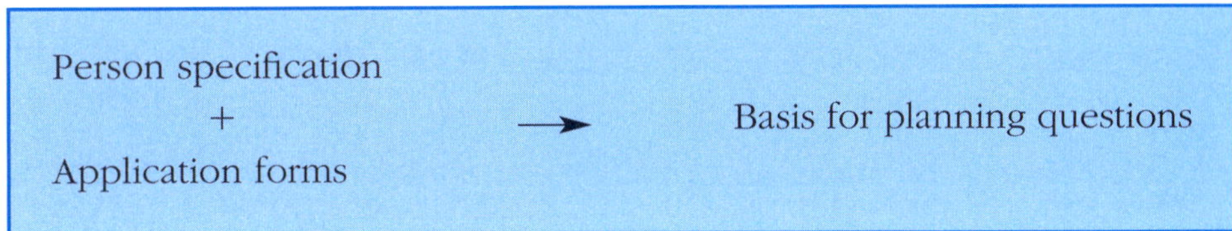

You do not have to put the same questions to every candidate – what's important is that you find out information to assess whether or not the candidate meets the person specification. This will enable you to compare candidates systematically and fairly. Although you are likely to have core questions that you ask each candidate, you will need to tailor questions specifically to each candidate in order to get the information you need.

In his book *What Color is Your Parachute*,[2] Richard Bolles recommends that candidates know the answers to the following five questions:

1 **Why are you here?** What's made you apply for this job
2 **What can you do for us?** Would you add to problems or be part of the solution
3 **What kind of a person are you?** We need to know if you will fit in or cause problems
4 **What distinguishes you from the nineteen other people who can do the same tasks that you can?** Are you better than the other candidates?
5 **Can I afford you?** If we decide we want you, can we offer enough for you to accept?

Richard Bolles believes that all employers want to know the answers to these questions although they will never be asked directly.

The basic skill of questioning is to ask questions which allow the candidate to give you plenty of information. For example:

- Tell me about ...
- Why did you ...
- How did you deal with ...
- What do you think ...
- What did you find to be ...

To find out more information you may need to probe into a specific area covered in the application. For example:

- Why did you decide that bringing in external support was appropriate?
- What made you change direction and move into fundraising?
- How useful did you find the project management course?

You may want to know what experience the candidates have of meeting some of the criteria of the person specification. For example:

- Can you give me an example of when you have had to work under pressure?
- What experience have you had of budgeting?
- What have been the main challenges involved in managing a dispersed team?

It may be appropriate to ask candidates how they would deal with hypothetical situations. For example:

- What would you do if you suspected bullying in your team?
- How would you deal with the demands of the new legislation?

There may also be a place for asking direct questions for checking facts. For example:

- How many people are in your team at the moment?
- What did you do in the six months between leaving Hanson's and starting in your current job?

ACTIVITY 21

The purpose of the interview is to assess the candidate's ability to do the job. It is the responsibility of the candidate to assess whether their personal circumstances will enable them to do the job as described in the job description.

Why should you **not** include the following questions?

Question	**Why not?**
Do you have any plans to start a family?	
Will your partner mind if you have to work late?	

FEEDBACK

Questions about children, marriage plans, intentions to start a family, potential difficulties of coping with working hours, etc. are evidence of bias against women. None of these factors have any bearing on a person's ability to meet a person specification.

Plan the structure of the interview

Planning the structure for the interview is essential. It ensures that everything is covered in a systematic way and that each candidate is treated fairly.

A typical structure might be:

- Introductions
- Opening – outline to the candidate how the interview will be structured
- Using the application form as a basis, get a clear picture of the applicant's experience ← pre-prepared questions needed here
- Clarify expectations of job description
- Focus on job description – any areas which you feel you need further information regarding the candidate's abilities ← pre-prepared questions needed here
- General questions to assess candidate's motivation and suitability for the post ← pre-prepared questions needed here
- Give candidate an opportunity to ask questions
- State what will happen next

If you are involved in a panel interview, make sure that you all:

1. agree the structure beforehand
2. decide beforehand who will ask which questions.

It's important to take notes during an interview to remind you of the candidate's responses. You should advise the candidate at the start of the interview that you'll be recording their responses. It's easier if there is more than one person interviewing. If you are interviewing on your own you will have to be brief; noting down words to jog your memory is often all that is needed.

Prepare the room

The layout of the room should be considered. It's often more practical for a panel of interviewers to sit behind a desk so they can refer to papers and take notes. However, this can be intimidating and may not be appropriate. The manner you adopt as an interviewer should be able to counteract any disadvantages of a formal room layout.

Check administrative details

For interviews to run smoothly ask yourself:

- have candidates been informed? (venue, time, any tests)
- has someone been briefed to welcome them on arrival?
- is there a suitable place for candidates to wait?
- is the room set up?
- has everybody who needs to know about the interviews been informed?
- are you able to meet any needs of candidates with disabilities?
- have you prepared all the necessary paperwork to take into the interview (e.g. job descriptions, questions, schedule of interview times, etc.)

COMMUNICATING DURING THE INTERVIEW

You need each candidate to perform to the best of their ability so you can make an accurate judgment on who is best for the job. Therefore, you need to put candidates at ease.

ACTIVITY 22

List three things you would either do or say in an interview to put a candidate at ease.

FEEDBACK

You may have included:

- Greet the candidate by name and thank them for coming
- Engaging in neutral conversation as you greet the candidate e.g. asking about their journey
- Using body language which helps to build a rapport e.g. smiling, nodding, using eye contact
- Explaining the structure of the interview so the candidate knows what's in store
- Help the candidate out if they are struggling with an answer

In addition to putting the candidate at ease, you need to focus on listening to their responses.

In Steven Covey's book, *The Seven Habits of Highly Effective People*,[3] he highlights that:

We typically seek first to be understood. Most people do not listen with the intent to understand; they listen with the intent to reply. They're either speaking or preparing to speak

He identifies four levels of listening:

1. **Ignoring** (pretending to listen)
2. **Selective listening** (listening to certain parts of what someone is saying)
3. **Attentive listening** (focusing on the words that are being said. However, experts in communication estimate that only 10 per cent of the meaning we convey is held within the words we choose; 90 per cent is made up of a combination of the *way* we say things and *body language*)
4. **Empathetic listening** (listening to understand).

According to Covey, empathetic listening involves listening not only with your ears but also with your eyes and heart. As an interviewer you need to listen empathetically to the replies of the candidate if you are to understand their responses.

Nature gave us one tongue
and two ears so we could
hear twice as much as we
speak.

Epictetus

ACTIVITY 23

Below is a 'How to listen' checklist adapted from *The Fifth Discipline Fieldbook*.[4] Consider each of the points and highlight any that you feel you don't instinctively do, either as an interviewer or when listening to people generally.

- Stop talking – you can't listen if you are talking.
- Imagine the other person's viewpoint.
- Look, act and **be** interested.
- Observe non-verbal behaviour (i.e. body language)
- Don't interrupt
- Listen between the lines for things left unsaid or unexplained – ask about them
- Make no judgment or criticism when listening
- Rephrase and reflect back what the other person has said at key points of the conversation to check understanding
- Stop talking – this is the first and last, because all other techniques of listening depend on it.

FEEDBACK

You may find it helpful to ask for feedback from someone who knows you in the work situation and whose viewpoint you respect. Probably the hardest of all the points is to listen without making judgment. It's very difficult to change a perception you have once you consider it to be fact.

"Man [has] always assumed that he was more intelligent than dolphins because he had achieved so much – the wheel, New York, wars and so on-while all the dolphins had ever done was muck about in the water having a good time.
But conversely, the dolphins had always believed that they were far more intelligent than man – for precisely the same reason."

Douglas Adams, *Hitchhiker's Guide to the Galaxy*

Making the decision – traps to avoid

A decision should be made immediately the assessment process has been completed. It must be based on objective assessment of all the evidence you have collected against the person specification. Use a candidate comparison form as we described for the shortlisting process, remembering to keep the documentation for up to six months in order to deal with any complaints about discrimination.

However, people have a tendency to recruit in their own image. In Section 1 we explored the disadvantages of this as well its unfairness. There are also a number of other traps for the unwary interviewer:

- Relying on 'first impressions'. We tend to form an impression about someone within about 20 seconds of meeting them. However, it's important to recognize that in a selection interview situation we have to suspend judgments until we have more reliable information.
- The 'halo' effect. This involves assuming that just because a candidate has one strong area then they will automatically be strong in all areas. Systematically exploring all aspects of the person specification can help to avoid the halo effect.
- After a long day of interviewing the first and last candidates tend to be easier to remember than the ones in the middle. One way round this is to ask candidates to bring a photograph or have a polaroid or digital camera available. Accurate note-taking and a realistic timetable will also help.

It is at this stage that references are most commonly checked.

REFERENCES

The purpose of a reference is to obtain factual information about a candidate. You should always let candidate's know that you will be approaching a referee.

References

- Don't ask referees for a general character reference only or subjective information as to a candidate's suitability for the job.
- References may be used to check factual evidence such as:
  - Job title
  - Details of responsibilities
  - Length of employment
  - Employment history
  - Qualifications
  - Time-keeping
  - Reason for leaving
  - General performance and development

(Source: www.eoc.org.uk (August 2004))

Communicating the outcome

Once you have made a decision you need to notify the successful candidate immediately – this is usually done by telephone. This would be followed by a formal offer in writing which includes all the terms and conditions of employment and instructions as to what to do next.

ACTIVITY 24

What actions do you need to take in line with your organization's procedures for appointing a new member of staff? Refer to the procedure or discuss with the Human Resource or Personnel department.

FEEDBACK

It's essential that you follow these procedures otherwise it's likely to cause administrative complications and difficulties.

You must also inform unsuccessful candidates. This is common courtesy. A delayed response gives a bad impression of you and your organization as well as it being unfair for candidates to be left hoping that they had got the job after the decision had been made.

Try to personalize your response to each candidate, if possible highlighting their positive points. If a personalized response is not possible, take care over your wording. For example:

'After careful consideration I regret to inform you that your application has not been successful. Please do not consider this a reflection upon your own skills and experience, but rather on the large and extremely high quality of the overall response which made the final selection very difficult.'

Candidates invest a lot of themselves into interviews, tests and assessment centres and your response can help to soften the impact of being rejected.

Learning summary

- The selection process includes:
  - creating a shortlist
  - assessing the shortlisted candidates
  - making a decision
  - communicating the outcome.
- It is essential that all the actions you take during the selection process follow your organization's policies and procedures.
- Shortlisting should take place systematically so that applications are assessed only against criteria in the person specification.
- If you are planning to use a work-related test make sure:
  - you are clear about which aspects of the person specification you are testing
  - the criteria you are assessing are critical to job success (otherwise there's no point putting the resources into a test)
  - you have a clear marking or rating system
  - any psychological tests are to be carried out only by people who are fully trained in their use and interpretation.

- Successful selection interviews are well-prepared. Make sure you:
  - prepare questions
  - prepare the room
  - plan the structure of the interview
  - check administrative details.
- Always try to put candidates at ease during the interview so they have the opportunity to show their potential
- Selection decisions must be based on objective assessment of all the evidence you have collected against the person specification
- As well as informing the successful candidate, make sure you also tell the unsuccessful applicants at the earliest opportunity.

Into the workplace

You need to:

- make selection decisions based on an objective assessment of the evidence.

References

1 Reported in the Financial Times Career Guide, 1989, for the United Kingdom
2 Bolles, R. (2004) *What Color is Your Parachute?* Ten Speed Press
3 Covey, S. (1992) *The Seven Habits of Highly Effective People*, Simon and Schuster.
4 Adapted from Senge, P. Kleiner, A., Roberts, C. et al. (1994) *The Fifth Discipline Fieldbook*, Nicholas Brearley Publishing Limited

Section 5 Induction and beyond – foundations of staff retention

Introduction

Staff turnover is a huge cost to most organizations. To recap from the start of the workbook:

- the average cost of turnover per employee in 2001 was £3462
- the average cost of turnover for a manager in 2001 was £5699.

Therefore, once you've appointed good employees the focus has to be on retaining them.

> **Retention difficulties**
>
> The proportion of organizations experiencing retention difficulties increased to 77 per cent during 2003 in the UK. Retention difficulties are most pronounced in the not-for-profit sector and private service industries. The manufacturing and production sector is least likely to report problems.
>
> ---
>
> Source: *Chartered Institute of Personnel and Development* Survey Report, June 2004, www.cipd.org.uk

There is a wide range of factors which influences why a person leaves or stays in a job. Some you will have little or no control over. For example, staff leaving due to factors such as:

- moving to higher paid jobs
- level of pay

- working hours
- family reasons
- redundancy
- retirement.

However, as a line manager the way you manage has a major impact on levels of job satisfaction within your team. For example, the way in which you communicate, whether or not you recognize and reward good performance, generally 'how things are done' in your team. In a nutshell, being good at managing people is the main contribution you can make to staff retention in your organization.

In this section we look at some of the ways you can influence the job satisfaction of the people you recruit in the early days. We look at the importance of:

- induction
- managing performance
- developing your team.

Induction

The impression that an employee gets of an organization in the early days can have a major impact on how long they stay.

CIPD research[1] has shown that:

- one in five new employees leave after less than six months
- half of the leaving population have only two years' service.

Percentage of employees....	2003 (%)
with 0–6 months' service	20
with 7–23 months' service	30
with 2–5 years' service	24
with more than 5 years' service	23

We highlighted the importance of managing expectations during the recruitment and selection process earlier in the workbook. Poor induction processes will also increase the likelihood of a new employee feeling dissatisfied and wanting to leave very quickly.

Induction has a number of purposes which include:

- learning about their own working environment
- learning about the organization
- an opportunity to adjust emotionally to a new workplace.

A clear, structured, planned induction enables a new employee to feel confident that:

1 their needs are being looked after
2 the organization values them.

ACTIVITY 25

Consider your own experiences of induction. On the continuum between 'totally' and 'not at all' mark the extent to which you felt:

	totally	**not at all**
■ Your needs were being looked after		
■ The organization valued you		

How did this affect your feelings towards working for the organization?

FEEDBACK

There may be some people who revel in being 'thrown into the deep end' but most appreciate an opportunity to discuss their induction programme before they start. It's often reassuring to at least know what will happen on Day 1.

There are no standard formats for an induction. Some organizations have set procedures to follow which act as a framework for line managers; others leave it totally to the line manager.

Often the best approach to planning an induction is to try and see things from the new employees point of view.

ACTIVITY 26

Put yourself in the shoes of someone who is about to join your team. What do you think they would expect from their induction process?

FEEDBACK

You may have included factors such as:

- to understand clearly what their role is
- to know what they are supposed to do
- to know how they will fit into the organization
- to know who they can ask for help
- to get to know their work colleagues
- not to have too much information thrown at them at once
- not to be left around wondering what to do
- to get on with some real work fairly soon.

You also need to think in terms of:

- What do I want to achieve? By when?
- What organizational information do I need to give?
- What do I need to do before this person starts?

Other people will have to know what's happening so that they can contribute. Ask yourself:

- What procedures do I have to follow to make sure everything goes smoothly? For example, informing Personnel, informing IT department, training department?
- How should I prepare the rest of the team? What do I expect from them?
- Do I need to alert anyone about this person's arrival, e.g. reception desk?

You are then in a position to design the induction programme. If the existing jobholder is still in the post, ask for their advice and ideas.

Ideally, a copy of the induction programme will have been sent to the new employee before Day 1.

For example:

		Who?
Day 1		
am	General introductions, shown round department, clarification of job role and employment details	Chris (line manager)
pm	Set up work station, introduction to files, work methods	Rapinder (mentor)
Day 2		
am	Attend corporate induction	Personnel
pm	■ Meet with Chris to discuss questions arising from corporate induction; set objectives for remainder of week	Chris
	■ Health and safety induction	Peter (health and Safety officer)

ACTIVITY 27

Below is a preparation induction checklist. Adapt it so that it is relevant to what you need to do.

Preparation for induction checklist

Have I:

- Informed personnel and given employment details ❑
- Booked relevant corporate training courses ❑
- Informed key people who will be affected by the appointment ❑
- Made sure that people involved in the induction are available at the required time ❑
- Discussed induction programme with the rest of the team ❑
- Drawn up an induction programme and sent it to new employee ❑
- Informed new employee of where to meet me on Day 1 ❑
- Alerted reception ❑
- Got ready all relevant documentation related to organization and department ❑
- Made sure any adjustments have been made if the new employee has a disability ❑

FEEDBACK

Planning and organising an induction demands commitment in terms of time and resources. However, managing it efficiently will lay the foundations for effective teamworking to develop.

Managing performance

As a line manager, one of your responsibilities is to manage the performance of your team. This involves a continuous cycle of setting and reviewing work objectives.

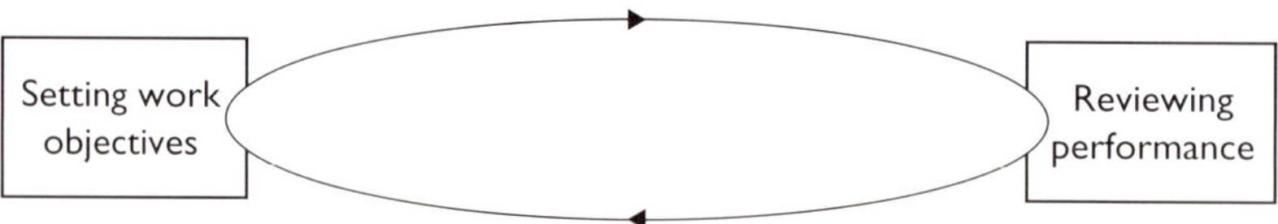

Organizations succeed by every employee's individual objectives being aligned and contributing to the overall objectives and direction of the organization.

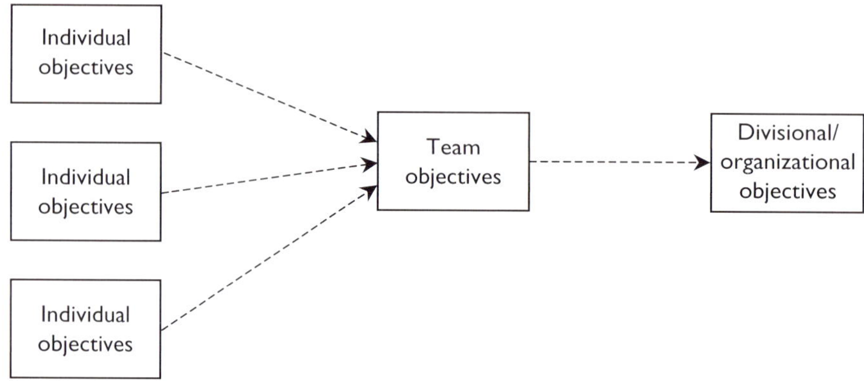

Effectively managing the performance of your team, however, is also a major contributory factor in job satisfaction, and ultimately, retention of members in your team. It's not just about ensuring that work objectives are set and met; equally important is that it's done in a way that motivates your team members.

The psychologist Abraham Maslow[2] identified that human behaviour is driven by five basic needs:

- Physiological needs (the need for food, water, shelter)
- Safety needs (the need to feel safe from danger)
- Social needs (the need for love, friendship and a feeling of belonging)
- Self-esteem needs (the need to feel good about ourselves)
- Self-actualization needs (the need to fulfill personal goals).

Maslow showed these needs in the form of a hierarchy with physiological needs at the bottom and the need for self-actualization at the top. Maslow's theory was that people were driven to fulfill the lower level needs before focusing on the higher level needs.

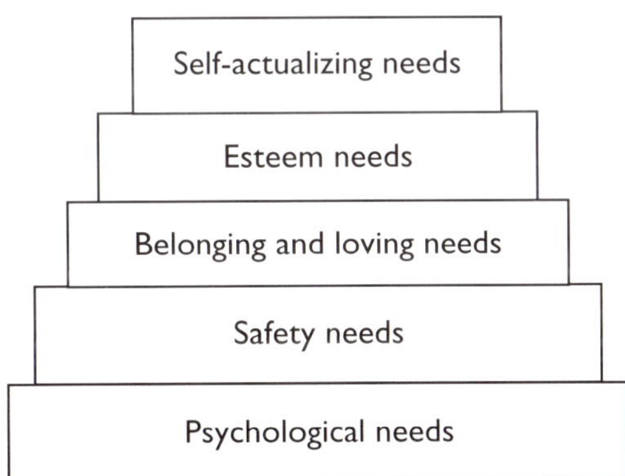

Figure 5.1 Maslow's hierarchy of needs (adapted from Maslow, A. A Theory of Human Motivation, Psychological Review, Vol. 50, 1943, p. 381.)

ACTIVITY 28

Which of Maslow's five 'needs' can you contribute to in the way you manage individual performance?

FEEDBACK

Managing performance effectively can contribute towards meeting a person's:

- **Need for self-esteem.** Recognizing achievement and giving praise is an essential part of the process of reviewing objectives.
- **Need for self-actualization.** A lot of personal satisfaction can be gained through achieving objectives, especially if those objectives were demanding or stretching.

Therefore, the way you manage performance can directly contribute to enable team members to meet basic human needs and, in turn, increase job satisfaction.

Managing performance begins during induction. Objectives should be set which begin the continuous cycle of performance management. It also gives you the opportunity to monitor performance and give constructive feedback before any bad habits set in.

Developing your team

ACTIVITY 29

Which statement do you agree with most strongly?

A Training staff increases their commitment to staying with the organization

B Training staff makes them more likely to leave for higher paid jobs elsewhere.

FEEDBACK

Research[3] has shown that:

- training which is paid for by the employer is less likely to result in people leaving than training paid for by either the employee or government
- training which is organizational-specific is less likely to result in staff leaving than training in transferable skills, e.g. management training.

Whatever your views you can almost guarantee that if employees feel neglected or undervalued it will impact on their job satisfaction and increase the likelihood of them leaving.

Therefore a feature of the way you manage performance should be to incorporate managing the development of team members.

Key point

Performance management should have two strands:

1. Objective setting and performance review
2. Ensuring team members have the skills and knowledge to meet the work objectives set

Identifying development opportunities

It's a common misconception that development is about attending a training course. Development is about unlocking people's potential. Training is one method of achieving development objectives but there are many others. For example, some of the main approaches include:

- coaching
- mentoring
- projects
- attachments
- work shadowing.

As a line manager, you need to introduce a culture of encouraging development into your team and embed it into performance management during induction.

Learning summary

- Staff turnover is a huge cost to most organizations.
- Job satisfaction affects staff turnover.
- The way you manage has a major impact on levels of job satisfaction within your team.
- You can increase job satisfaction, and impact of staff retention by:
  - Providing a good induction programme to new recruits
  - Effectively managing the individual performance of members of your team
  - Integrating development and training into the way you manage the performance of your team.

Into the workplace

You need to:

- Provide a good induction to new members of your team
- Recognize the importance of managing your team's performance on retention.

References

1 Recruitment, Retention and Turnover, Survey Report June 2004, www.cipd.org.uk

2 Maslow, A.H. (1943) A Theory of Human Motivation, *Psychological Review*, Vol. 50, p. 381

3 Green, F., Felstead, A., Mayhew, K. and Pick, A. (2000) The impact of training on labour mobility: individual and firm-level evidence from Britain, *British Journal of Industrial Relations*, 38(2), 261–275

Information toolbox

General information

Cook, M. (2004) *Personnel Selection Adding Value Through People*, Wiley

Dale, M. (2003) *Managers' Guide to Recruitment and Selection*, Kogan Page

Evans, A. (2001) *Staff Recruitment and Retention: Strategies for Effective Action*, Chandos Publishing

Fowler, A. (2000) *Writing Job Descriptions*, Chartered Institute of Personnel and Development

Hindle, T. (1998) *Interviewing Skills*, Dorling Kindersley

MacDonald, J. and Riley, J. (1999) *Successful Recruitment in a Week*, Institute of Management Foundation, Hodder and Stoughton

ACAS provides information, advice and training and works with employers and employees to solve problems and improve performance in the workplace www.acas.org.uk

Diversity, equality and the law

Commission for Racial Equality www.cre.gov.uk

Disability Rights Commission (DRC). The DRC gives advice and information and helps solve problems with employers, service providers and disabled people www.drc.org.uk

Equality Direct offer advice for employers on a wide range of equality issues and also provide a telephone service. www.equalitydirect.org.uk Tel: 0845 600 3444

Job Accommodation Network is a free consulting service designed to increase the employability of people with disabilities in the USA www. jan.wvu.edu/

Leighton, P. and Proctor, G. (2003) *Recruiting Within the Law*, CIPD

Psychological tests

British Psychological Society, www.bps.org.uk Tel: 0116 254 9568

Psychometric Tests and Racial Equality: A Guide for Employers, Commission for Racial Equity 1992

Edenborough, R. (1999) *Using Psychometrics: A Practical Guide to Testing and Assessment*, Kogan Page

EOC (1997) *Avoiding Sex Bias in Selection Testing: Guidance for Employers*, Equal Opportunities Commission

CMI Management Information Centre

One of the benefits of membership of the Chartered Management Institute is free and unlimited access to a library containing more than 30,000 books and 40,000 articles. The Institute provides tailored reading lists on any management topic requested. These are usually e-mailed to you on the same day as you request them. All books and articles are posted first-class and are therefore received the day after ordering.

Telephone: 01536 207307 Website: www.managers.org.uk